ISBN-13: 9798859032549
ISBN-10: 1477123456

Cover design by: Mariella Peters
Library of Congress Control Number: 2018675309
Printed in the United States of America

I0409802

To my incredible support team,

I dedicate this book to my loving children and my amazing husband, who have been the driving force behind my journey as an author. Your unwavering belief in me and your constant encouragement have been the cornerstone of my success.

To my children, Calee, Haelyn, and Hayden, your boundless curiosity, imagination, and belief in God inspire me every day. You remind me of the power of storytelling and the joy that can be found in every adventure. Thank you for sharing in my dreams and for understanding when Mommy disappeared into the world of words.

To my dearest husband, Tom, your unwavering support, patience, and love have been my rock throughout this writing process. You have believed in me even when I doubted myself, and your words of encouragement have lifted me up during moments of uncertainty. Thank you for standing by my side, cheering me on, and sharing this remarkable journey together.

This book is a testament to our bond as a family and the incredible strength we draw from one another. You have sacrificed your time and made countless sacrifices to ensure that I could pursue my passion for writing and entrepreneurship. Your belief in me has given me the courage to chase my dreams fearlessly, and I am forever grateful.

To my support team, my kids, and my amazing husband, thank you for being the guiding light in my life. Your love, laughter, and unwavering belief in me have made this book possible. May these pages be a tribute to our shared adventures and a reminder of the profound love that fills our home. Also, I want to thank you, God, for the life you have blessed me with, for the talents and gifts you have bestowed upon me, and for the opportunities that have shaped me into the person I am today. Your divine grace has carried me through the challenges and triumphs, reminding me of your infinite love and boundless mercy.

With all my love,

Mommy aka Mariella Peters

CONTENTS

CRYPTOCURRENCY

ADVENTURES

Exploring the World of Digital Money!

INTRODUCTION

Welcome, young adventurers, to the exciting world of cryptocurrency! In this interactive eBook, we'll embark on a journey to discover what cryptocurrency is all about and how it can be both fun and fascinating. Get ready to unlock the secrets of digital money and embark on thrilling crypto adventures!

CHAPTER 1: THE AMAZING

WORLD OF MONEY

Money helps us trade and exchange goods and services. It comes in different forms and has been used throughout history in various ways. Long ago, people used to barter, trading goods directly without using money. They exchanged things like food, tools, and clothes for other items they needed. Later on, people started using shells, stones, and precious metals as money. Money is like a magic token that represents value. When you have money, you can use it to obtain something you like, such as toys, books, or ice cream. It's like having a special key that can unlock the things you want.

Money comes in different forms, such as coins and paper bills, which have special designs and numbers on them representing different values. Another form is a digital currency, existing on computers and the internet. Digital money is like a secret code or number that represents value. People can use digital money to buy things online or sometimes even in physical stores.

Money, whether physical or digital, is crucial because it helps us trade and buy the things, we need to live comfortable lives. It's a way for people to share and exchange what they have with others. So, the next time you see coins or paper bills, or use a digital payment app, remember that it's all money. It's a special tool that helps us obtain the things we want and need.

CHAPTER 2: EXPLORING

THE CONCEPT OF

DIGITAL CURRENCY

In today's modern world, we have something amazing called digital currency. It's a special type of money that doesn't have a physical form like coins or paper bills. Instead, it exists only in the digital realm, just like the games we play or the videos we watch on a computer or tablet.

Imagine having a special kind of money that you can use on the internet. It's like having your own secret treasure chest that you can open whenever you want to buy something online. With digital currency, you can explore online stores, find cool toys, books, or even treats, and use your digital money to make the purchase.

Using digital currency is really convenient because you don't need to carry around physical coins or bills. You can simply use your computer or a digital device to make a payment. It's like having a magical wallet inside your computer that holds your digital coins, and with just a few clicks, you can send them to someone else or use them to buy something exciting.

Digital currency has become popular because it's fast and easy to use. You can make transactions with people from all around the world without worrying about different types of money or exchange rates. It's like a universal language of money that everyone online understands. Or do they?

CHAPTER 3: BEING

RESPONSIBLE WITH

DIGITAL CURRENCY

J ust like with any form of money, it's important to be responsible and use digital currency wisely. When using digital currency, it's crucial to prioritize safety and security. Here are some key points to keep in mind:

Seek guidance: Before using digital currency, always consult with a grown-up or your parents. They can provide valuable advice and ensure you understand the potential risks and precautions associated with using digital currency.

Trusted platforms: Use trusted websites or apps when engaging with digital currency. Stick to well-known and reputable platforms that have a track record of security and user protection.

Privacy and security: Be mindful of your personal information and digital security. Protect your passwords and private keys by using strong, unique passwords and enabling additional security measures like two-factor authentication.

Scams and phishing: Be vigilant against scams and phishing attempts. Avoid clicking on suspicious links or providing personal information to unknown sources. Educate yourself about common scams and learn how to identify and avoid them.

Responsible spending: Treat digital currency as you would treat physical money. Be mindful of your spending habits and avoid impulsive purchases. Develop good financial habits and understand the value of your digital currency before making any transactions.

CHAPTER 4: THE PIONEER

CRYPTOCURRENCY

B itcoin is the pioneering cryptocurrency that introduced the world to the concept of decentralized digital currency. Here are some key points about Bitcoin:

Blockchain technology: Bitcoin operates on a decentralized technology called blockchain. Blockchain is a transparent and secure digital ledger that records all Bitcoin transactions. It ensures transparency, security, and immutability of the transaction history.

Decentralization: Bitcoin is not controlled by any central authority or government. It operates on a peer-to-peer network, allowing users to send and receive Bitcoin directly without intermediaries. This decentralized nature gives Bitcoin its unique features and eliminates the need for traditional banking systems.

Global accessibility: Bitcoin enables seamless transactions across borders. It doesn't rely on traditional banking systems or fiat currencies, making it accessible to anyone with an internet connection, regardless of their location.

Limited supply: Bitcoin has a limited supply, with only 21 million coins that can ever exist. This scarcity contributes to its value and has led to Bitcoin's reputation as a store of value and potential hedge against traditional financial systems.

CHAPTER 5: EXPLORING

ALTCOINS

A ltcoins, or alternative cryptocurrencies, refer to any digital currency other than Bitcoin. Here are some key points about altcoins:

Diverse features: Altcoins offer a wide range of features and purposes beyond being a medium of exchange. They are designed to address specific needs and challenges in the digital world. For example, Ethereum enables the creation of decentralized applications and smart contracts, while other altcoins focus on privacy, scalability, or specialized use cases.

Innovation and experimentation: Altcoins foster innovation and experimentation in the cryptocurrency space. Developers and entrepreneurs create new altcoins to explore different ideas, technologies, and functionalities, pushing the boundaries of what's possible with digital currency.

Investment opportunities: Altcoins provide investment opportunities for those looking beyond Bitcoin. Some altcoins have experienced significant growth and have the potential for high returns. However, it's important to conduct thorough research and understand the risks associated with altcoin investments.

CHAPTER 6: THE EVER-EVOLVING CRYPTO LANDSCAPE

T he world of cryptocurrency is dynamic and constantly evolving. Here are some key points about the ever-evolving crypto landscape:

Ongoing development: Cryptocurrencies continue to evolve

through ongoing development and innovation. Developers and communities actively work on improving existing cryptocurrencies and creating new ones, introducing new features, addressing scalability issues, and enhancing security.

Diverse applications: Cryptocurrencies are not limited to financial transactions. They have the potential to revolutionize various industries and applications. For example, blockchain technology, the foundation of cryptocurrencies, is being explored for use cases such as supply chain management, healthcare, voting systems, and more. The versatility of cryptocurrencies opens up a world of possibilities for innovative solutions and decentralized systems.

Regulation and mainstream adoption: As cryptocurrencies gain popularity, governments and regulatory bodies are developing frameworks to regulate their use. This process aims to ensure consumer protection, prevent illegal activities, and foster the mainstream adoption of cryptocurrencies. The level of regulation varies across different countries, and it's essential to stay informed about the legal landscape in your jurisdiction.

Market volatility: The cryptocurrency market is known for its volatility, with prices fluctuating significantly in short periods. This volatility presents both opportunities and risks for investors and traders. It's crucial to approach cryptocurrency investments with caution, conduct thorough research, and consider your risk tolerance.

CHAPTER 7: EMBRACING

THE FUTURE OF FINANCE

AND TECHNOLOGY

T he world of cryptocurrency is continually evolving and shaping the future of finance and technology.

Here are some key points about embracing the future of crypto:

Financial empowerment: Cryptocurrencies empower individuals by providing greater control over their financial assets. With cryptocurrencies, you can be your own bank, transact directly with others, and access financial services without traditional intermediaries. This financial empowerment fosters financial inclusion and accessibility.

Technological advancements: Cryptocurrencies are at the forefront of technological advancements, such as blockchain technology and decentralized applications. These innovations have the potential to revolutionize various industries, streamline processes, enhance security, and enable new business models.

Community and collaboration: The cryptocurrency ecosystem thrive on community participation and collaboration.

Communities of developers, enthusiasts, and users work together to improve cryptocurrencies, build decentralized applications, and drive adoption. Engaging with the community can provide valuable insights, learning opportunities, and connections within the crypto space.

Lifelong learning: The world of cryptocurrencies is complex and ever-evolving. Embracing the future of crypto requires a commitment to lifelong learning. Stay curious, explore new technologies and concepts, follow industry news and developments, and engage with educational resources to deepen your understanding of the crypto landscape.

CONCLUSION

Congratulations, brave crypto adventurers! You've completed your journey through the world of cryptocurrency. Now you have a solid understanding of what digital money is, how it works, and why it's so exciting. Remember, the world of crypto is always evolving, so stay curious, keep learning, and who knows what incredible crypto adventures await you in the future!

Keep exploring, keep learning, and keep embracing digital currency. The crypto world awaits you, young adventurers!

DISCLAIMER

The information provided is for educational purposes only and should not be construed as financial or investment advice. It is essential to consult with a qualified financial professional or advisor before making any investment decisions. Remember, investing involves risks, and there is no guarantee of returns.

ABOUT THE AUTHOR

Mariella Peters

Mariella Peters is a passionate author and seasoned professional with a diverse range of skills and experiences. From a young age, she discovered her love for writing and storytelling, and her dedication to the craft has driven her to become the author of this informative book, "Cryptocurrency Adventures, Exploring The World of Digital Money!"

DIGITAL
MILLIONAIRE
A Digital Business Firm

With a lifelong passion for writing, Mariella Peters has honed her storytelling abilities over the years, allowing her skills to come alive on the pages of her books. Her commitment to her craft is evident in the material she creates.

Beyond her writing pursuits, Mariella Peters is also a successful financial consultant that specialize in crypto investing. As a motivational speaker and leadership development consultant. Armed with a degree from Albany University's prestigious business school, she was recruited by one of the top accounting firms in the world. Her expertise and passion for financial consulting led her to now deliver informational presentations/ speeches that helps companies succeed and thrive.

When the onset of the Covid pandemic, Mariella Peters made the decision to prioritize her family and chose to stay home to care for her children. During this transformative period, she recognized the need for change and embarked on a journey of personal growth and entrepreneurship.

Today, Mariella Peters is excited to explore her diverse skill set and pursue various avenues of entrepreneurship, with writing being a central focus. Through her writing, she aims to captivate readers and transport them into imaginative and informational worlds filled with intrigue, emotion, and unforgettable learning experiences.

We invite you to delve into "Cryptocurrency Adventures, Exploring The World of Digital Money!" and embark on a educational journey crafted by the talented and passionate author, Mariella Peters. Stay tuned for more of her engaging works as she continues to share her storytelling and educational teaching gifts with the world.

Thank you for your support, and happy reading!